Adult Coloring Series

People Dreams #2

The Dancers

by
KerryDean

Released for sale
in support of the RocketHub Project:
http://bit.ly/1HCuLk9

We *APPRECIATE* your creations,
and Want to Show Them
from the Online Mountain Tops!
Attach a scan of your favorite and email to:

Info@**TeamWorx-Inc**.com

A sense of humility requires us to refrain
from trumpeting our perfection, so
IF you have any feedback, criticism or praise
to share, simply let us know at:
Info@TeamWorx-Inc.com

And IF IF IF you don't like this coloring book,
we'll quickly refund your fee.
Just email us at guarantee@TeamWorx-Inc.com

These were all drawn from life, between 1985 and 1990; in Pattaya and Bangkok,
Thailand, during the artist's Toulouse Lautrec phase.

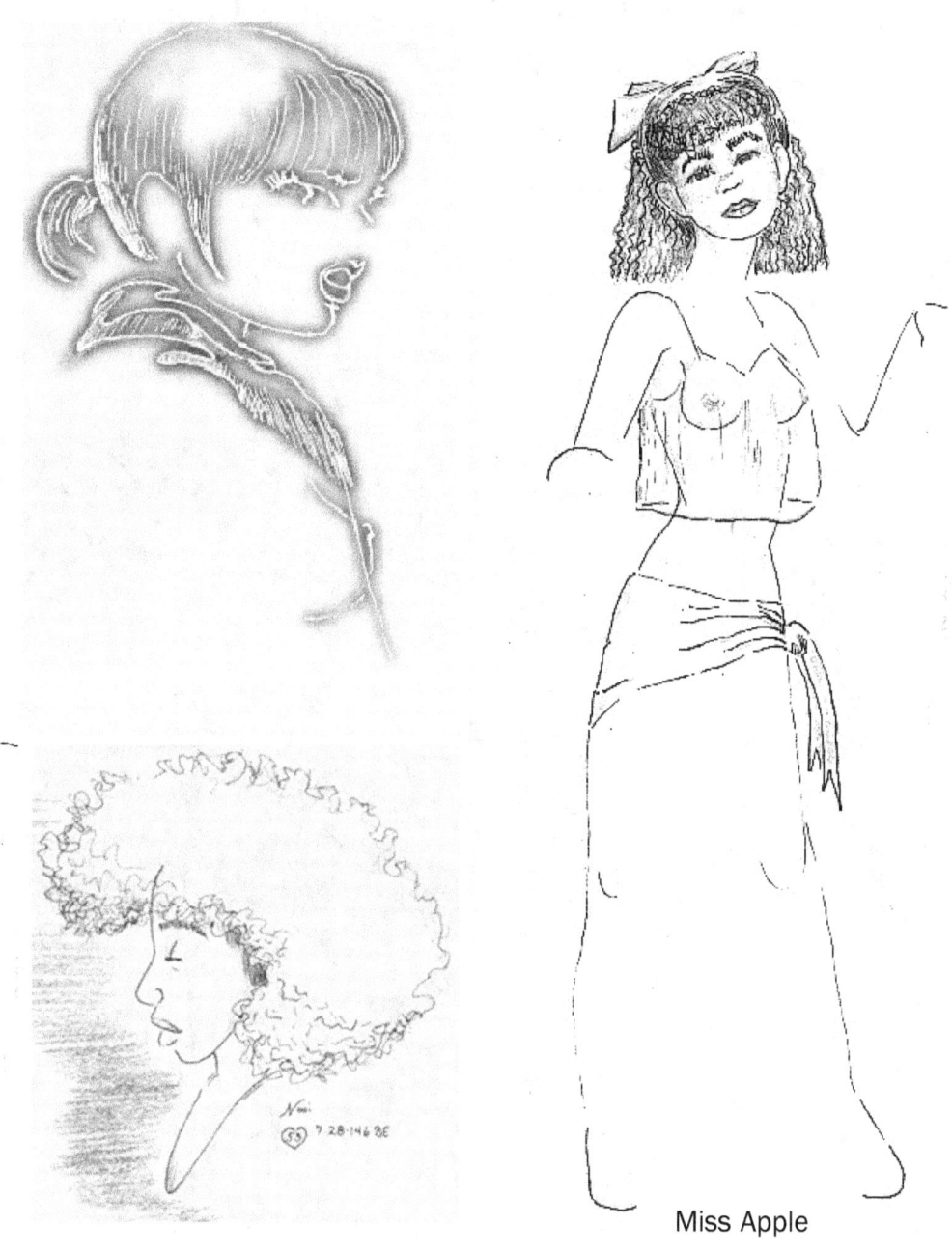

Miss Apple

This is what you get, but all the rest here are UNCOLORED,
just waiting for YOUR artistic touch to fill in color and details.
(Then see Appendix for some stories behind the faces.)

Athletic, fit, Miss Bunny was a finely-tuned dancer...

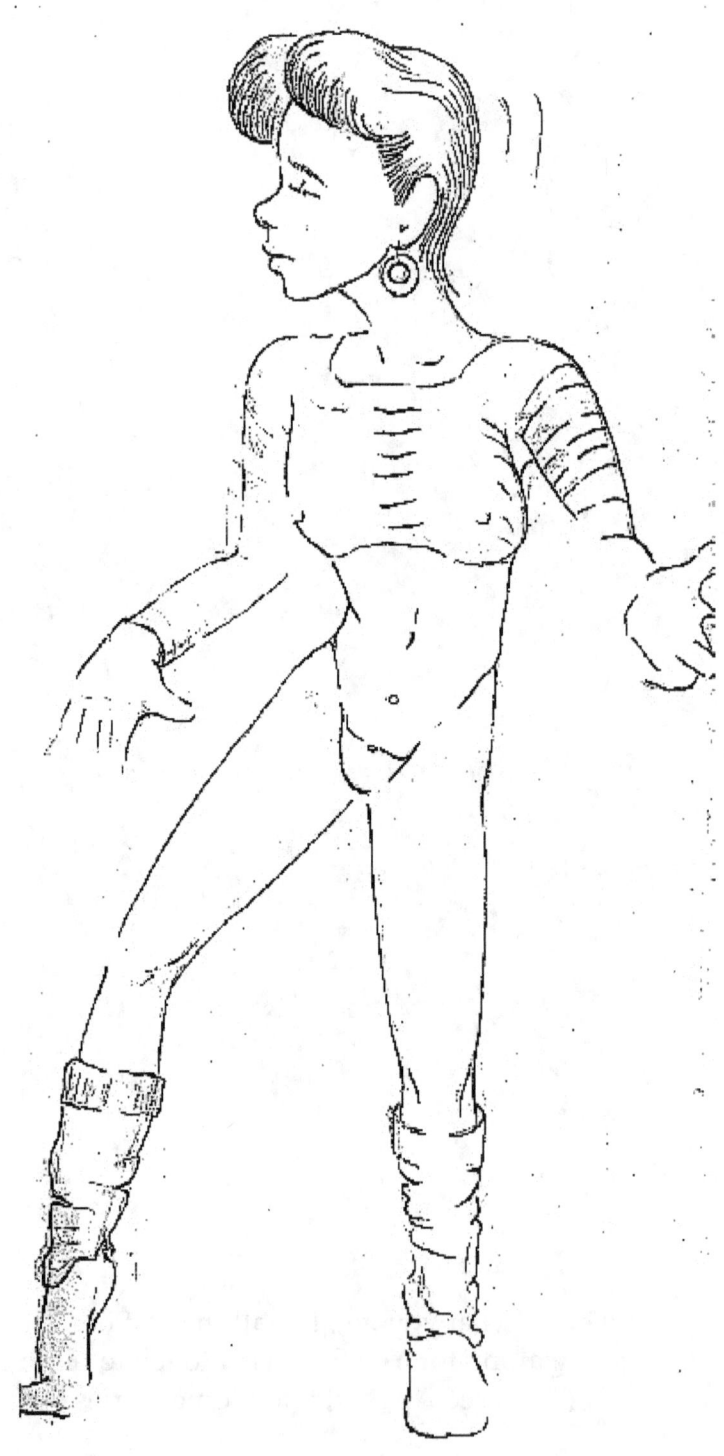

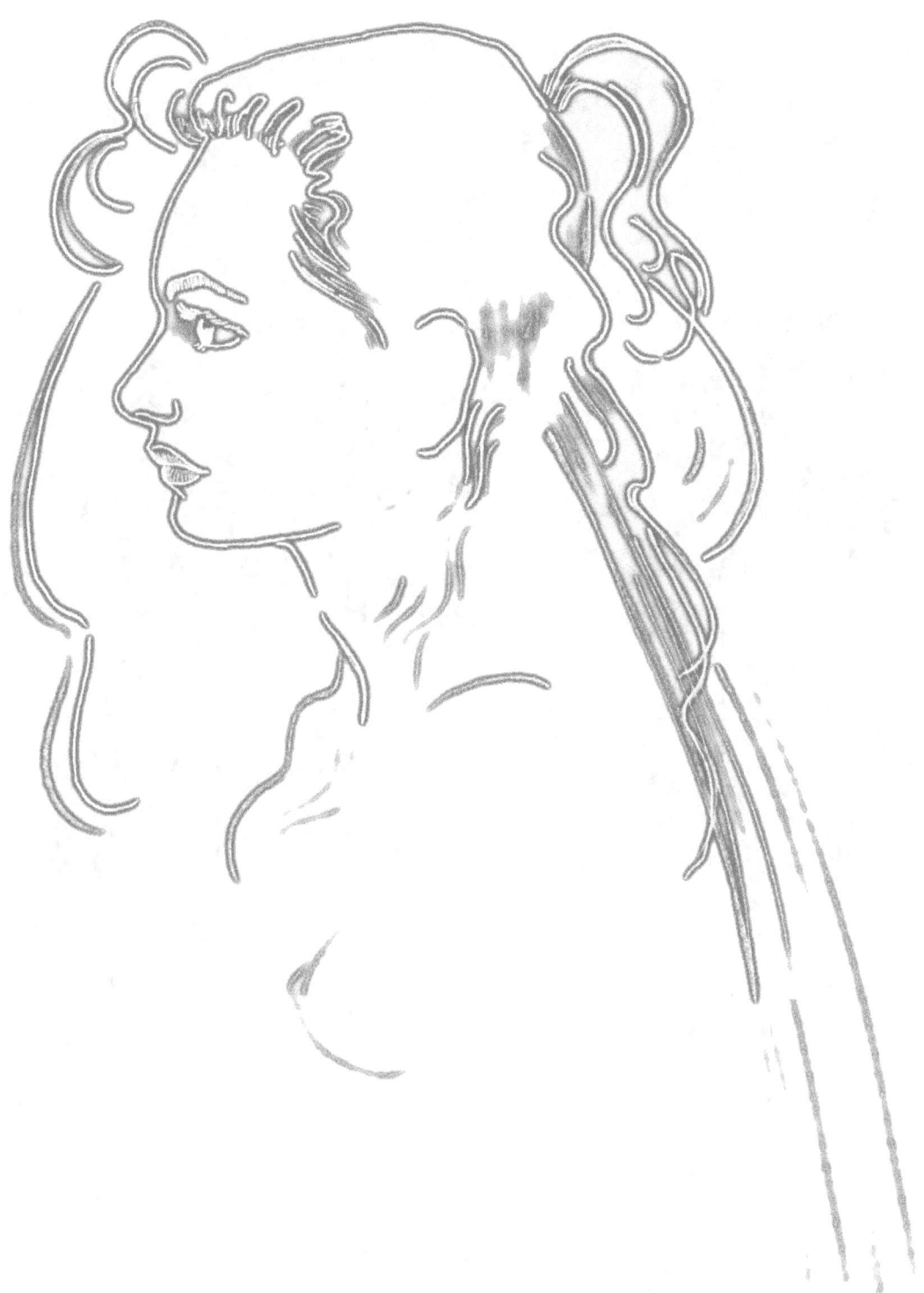

Danced at a private club off Sukumwit, named Annies.

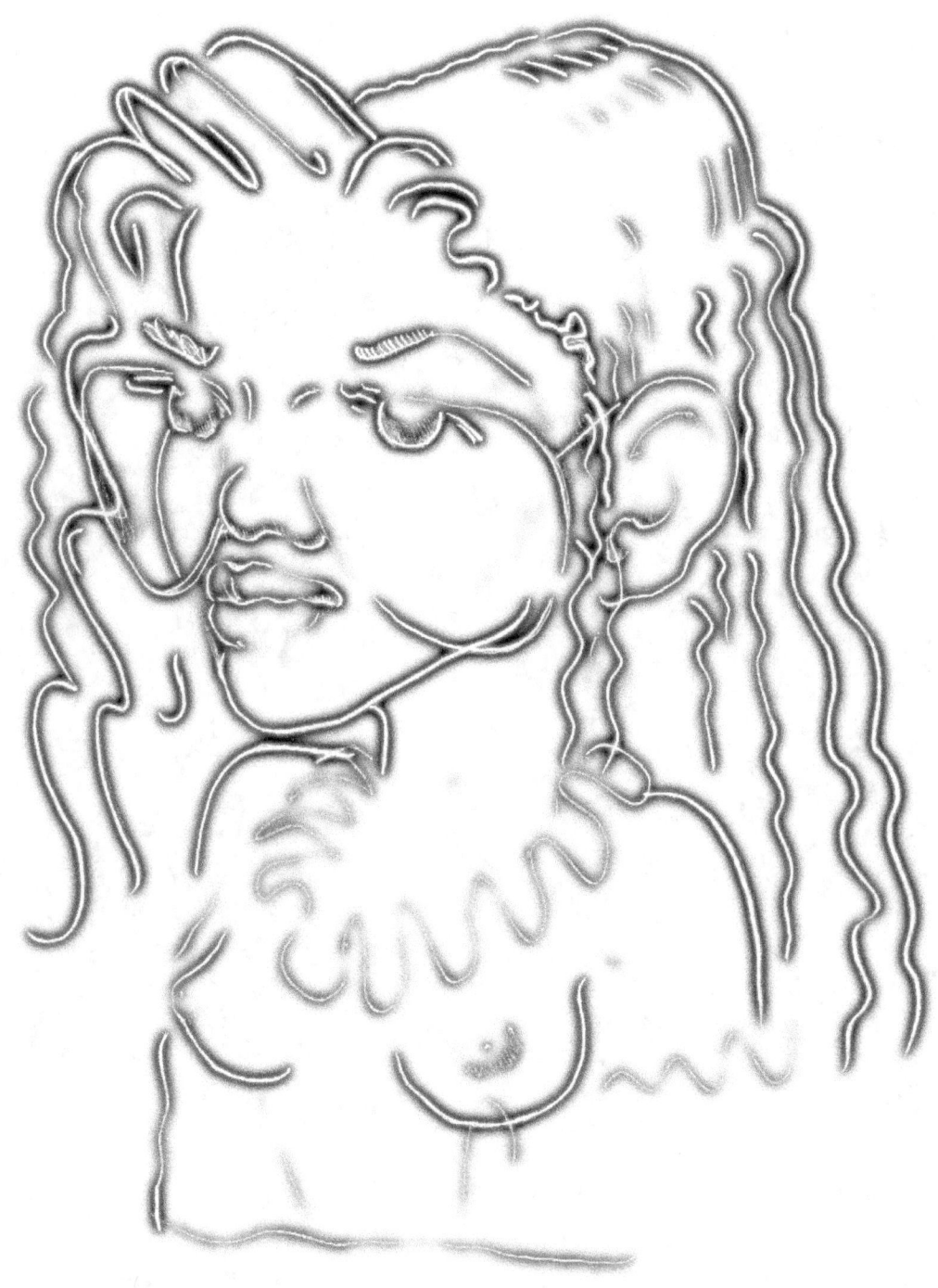

And another from Annie's... yes, her glasses WERE that big!

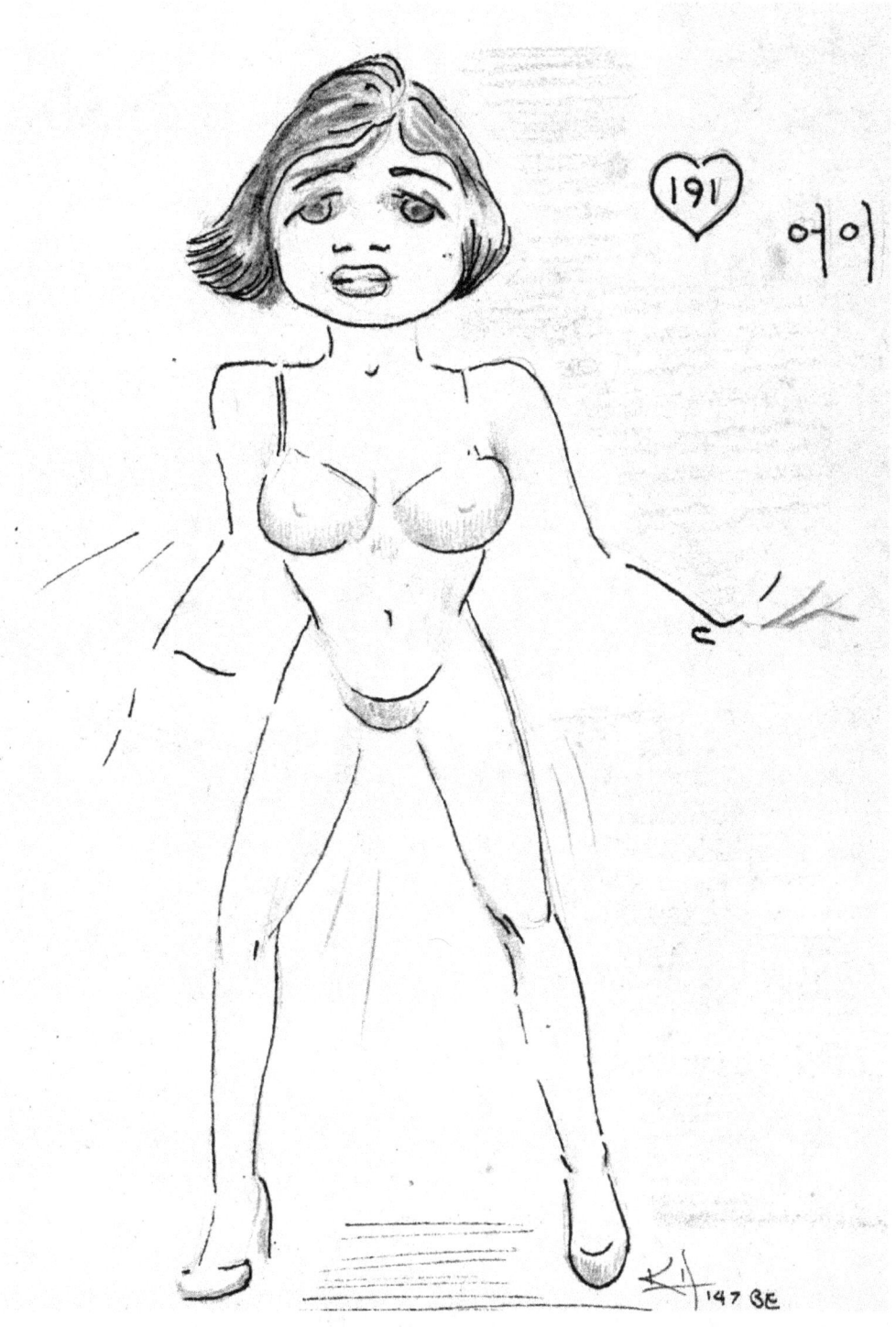

Miss Awe-ee... from Pattaya/Jomtien

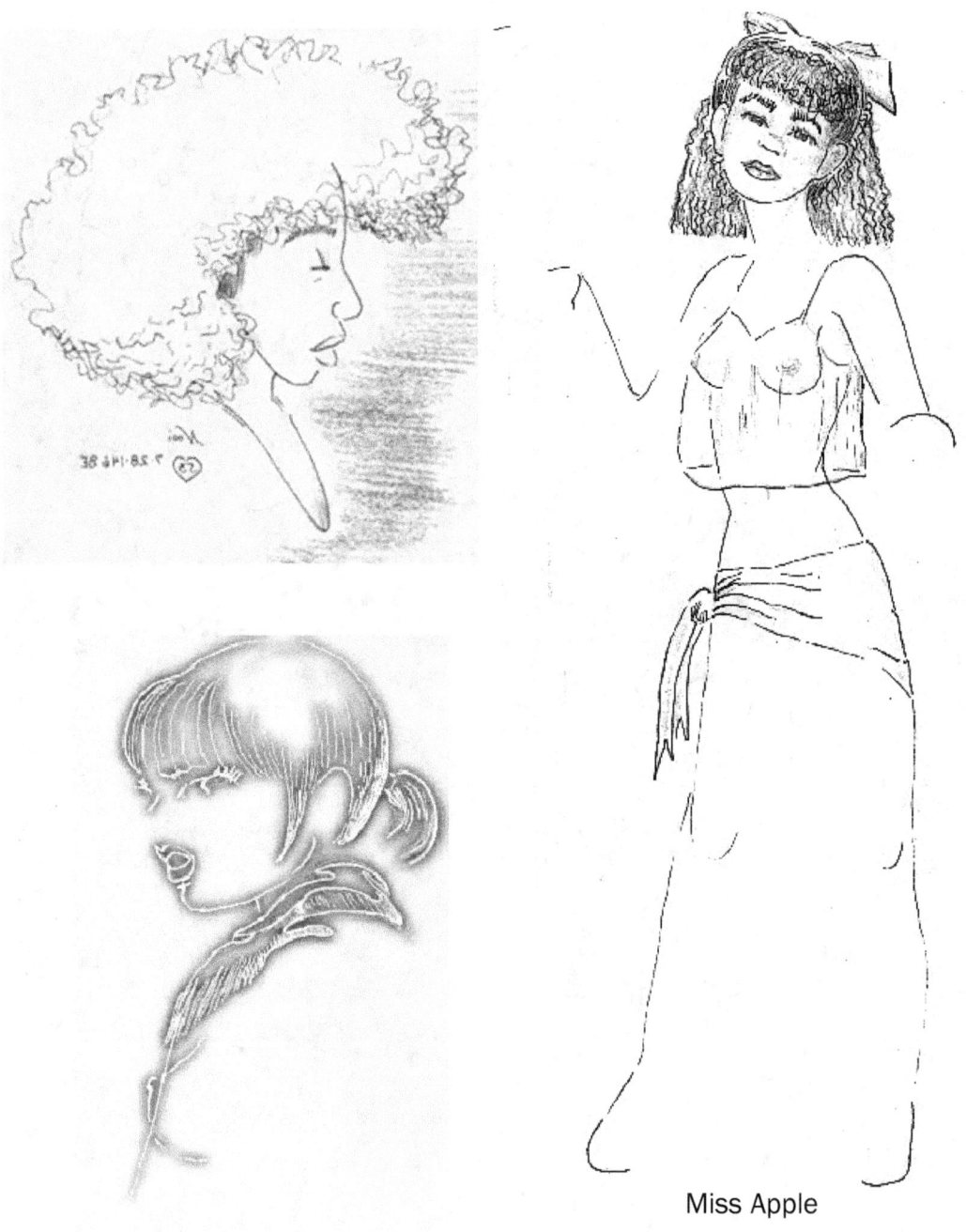

Miss Apple

Hey, here is the de-colorized version of these for you. Miss Apple
is the one on the right.

From Pattaya's most 'successful' GoGo bar, Baby GoGo, here's
Miss Nawy.

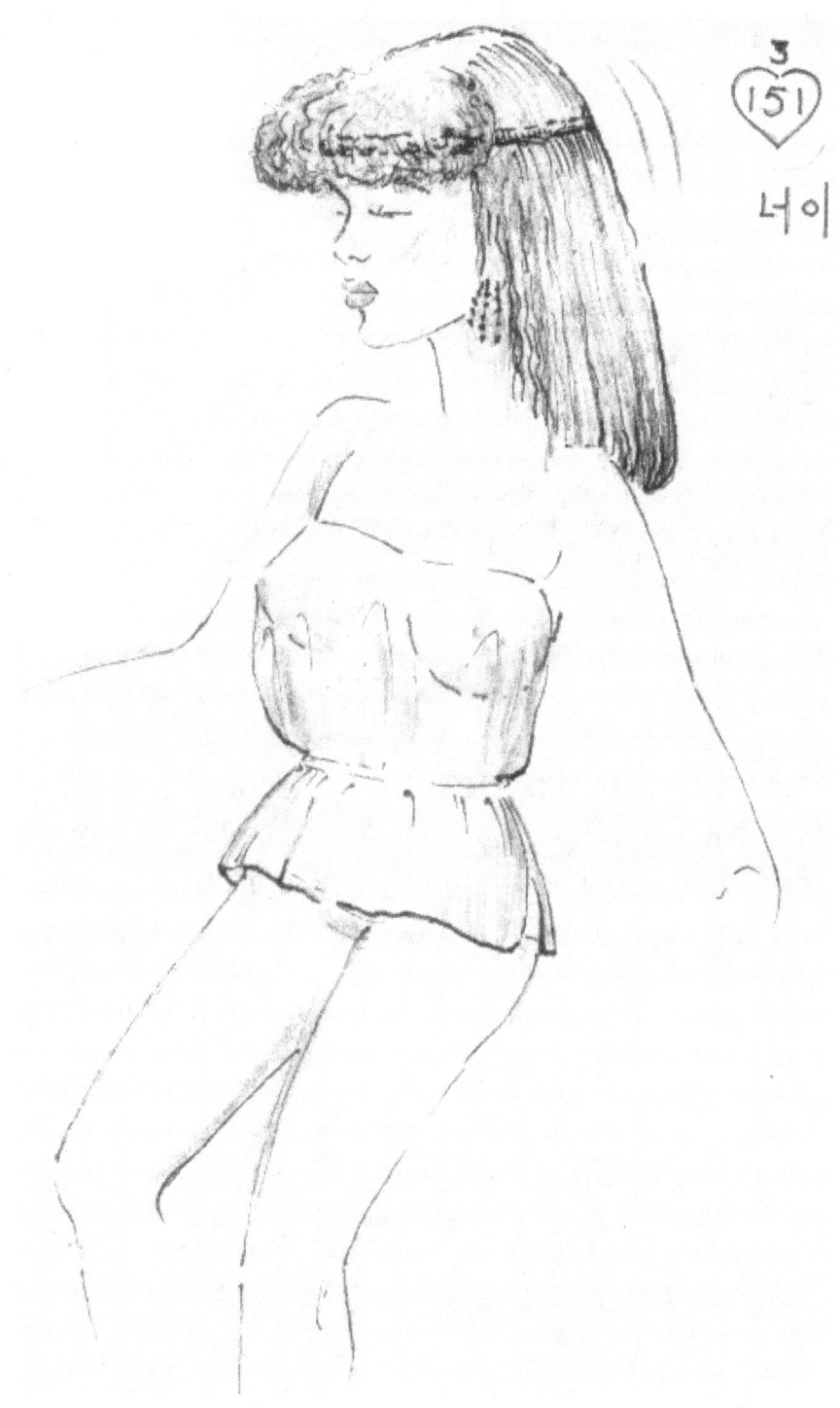

1. Use colored pencils, water-soluble is best, because when you've finished pencil-coloring, you can *-if you want to-* go back with a fine water-color paint-brush with water-damp only and play with slowly merging various patches and colors...

2. Turn off your desktop, your phone, tablet, pad and tin-can speaker-phones, so you have some actual QUIET for a few moments...

3. Go to your favorite page and start there. Go from lighter colors to darker, so you avoid muddy, brown-black finished pictures, but other than this... *anything goes!*

4. Begin coloring. Note how different strokes give you different textures. Experiment. Play! Pencil point size and shape also affect your picture. Up to down? Down to up? Diagonal? Fine point? Wedge-shaped? Blunt?

5. You may note after a few moments, that you're focusing on colors, light, shapes, hope, life, justice, courtesy and a host of other GOOD FEELINGS. *Enjoy*. These are your normal, natural birthright feelings, and you have every right to feel this way. When you notice you feel more creative, content, imaginative, playful or excited, REJOICE! You deserve these feelings!

Remember that coloring here, like writing a love-letter or making acoustic music or singing in a choir or growing in love, IS the payoff of the exercize and needs no permission or rationalizing.

"Art is a human act. **Art is Risky**. Generous. Courageous. Provocative. You can be perfect, or you can make art. You can keep track of what you will get in return for your effort, or you can make art. You can enjoy the status quo, or you can **make art**." Erik Wahl

For other Adult Coloring Books by Karridine, with original line-drawings from life, see the '*People Dreams*' series.

The Cleanup Crew Project:

RocketHub.com
http://www.rockethub.com/59614

This coloring book for adults is like many other adult coloring books that grew out of the Art Therapy movement and really became popular around 2013CE.

Created to help fund the indie film (for a possible series), this book also helps people understand some of the difficulties for people seeking racial harmony in World War II.

The **Nazi**onal Socialists (Nazis) OPENLY said that their 'white' race was a superhuman race and deserved to control, rule over and benefit from all other 'sub-humans', which included blacks, Asians, ALL-non-whites, Gypsies, Slavic, Jews, Arabic homosexual and retarded... and the list went on and on!

So '**Cleanup Crew**' pays homage to all who fought against the racist, destructive goals of the National *Socialists* and their allies.

http://www.rockethub.com/59614
Donate Today!

http://bit.ly/1HCuLk9

Find on Amazon the adult coloring book:
Cleanup Crew
for more coloring pleasure!

Miss Bug-Eyes

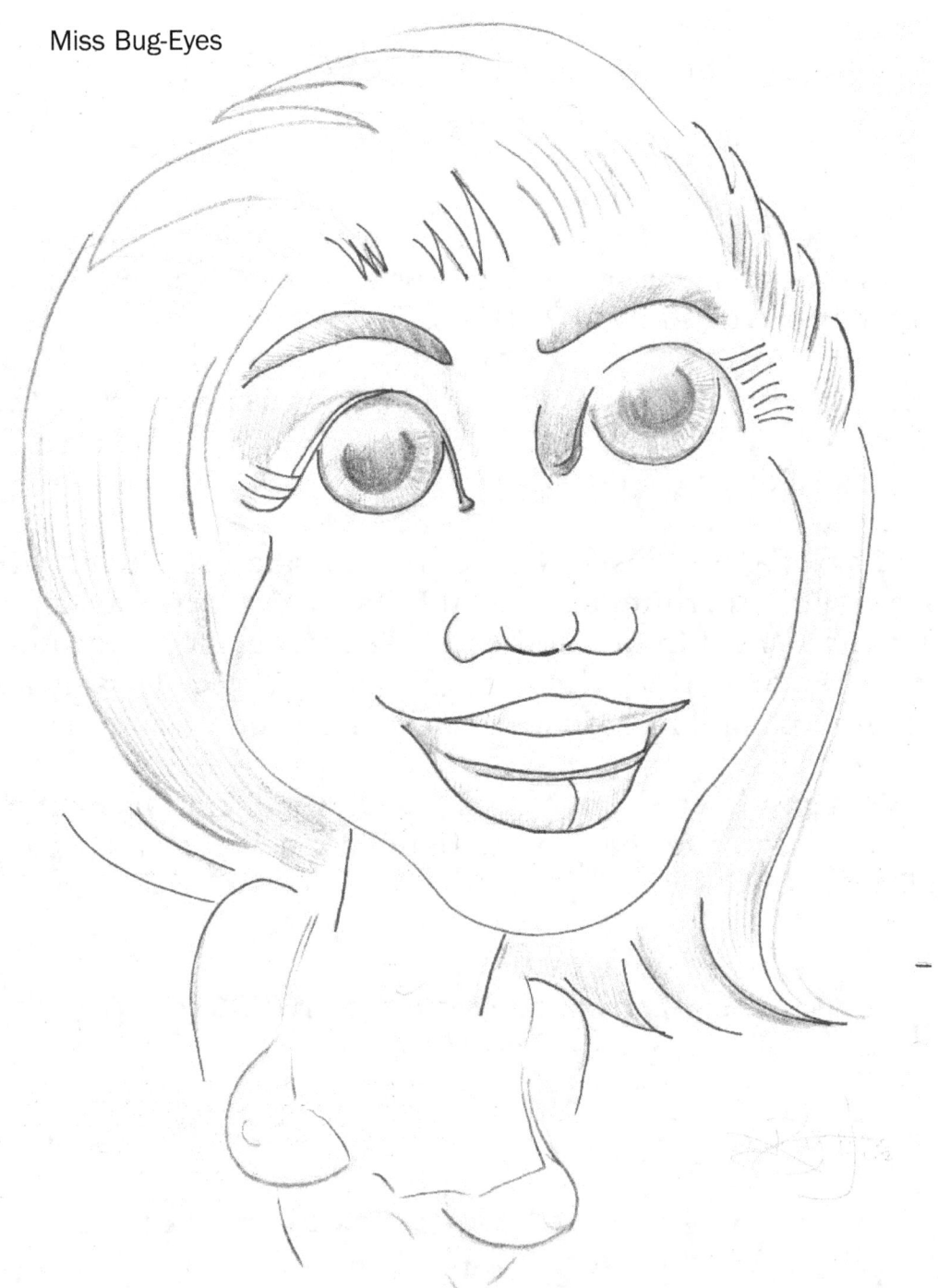

Outside her club, cheerful and inviting...
'Wanna come inside?'

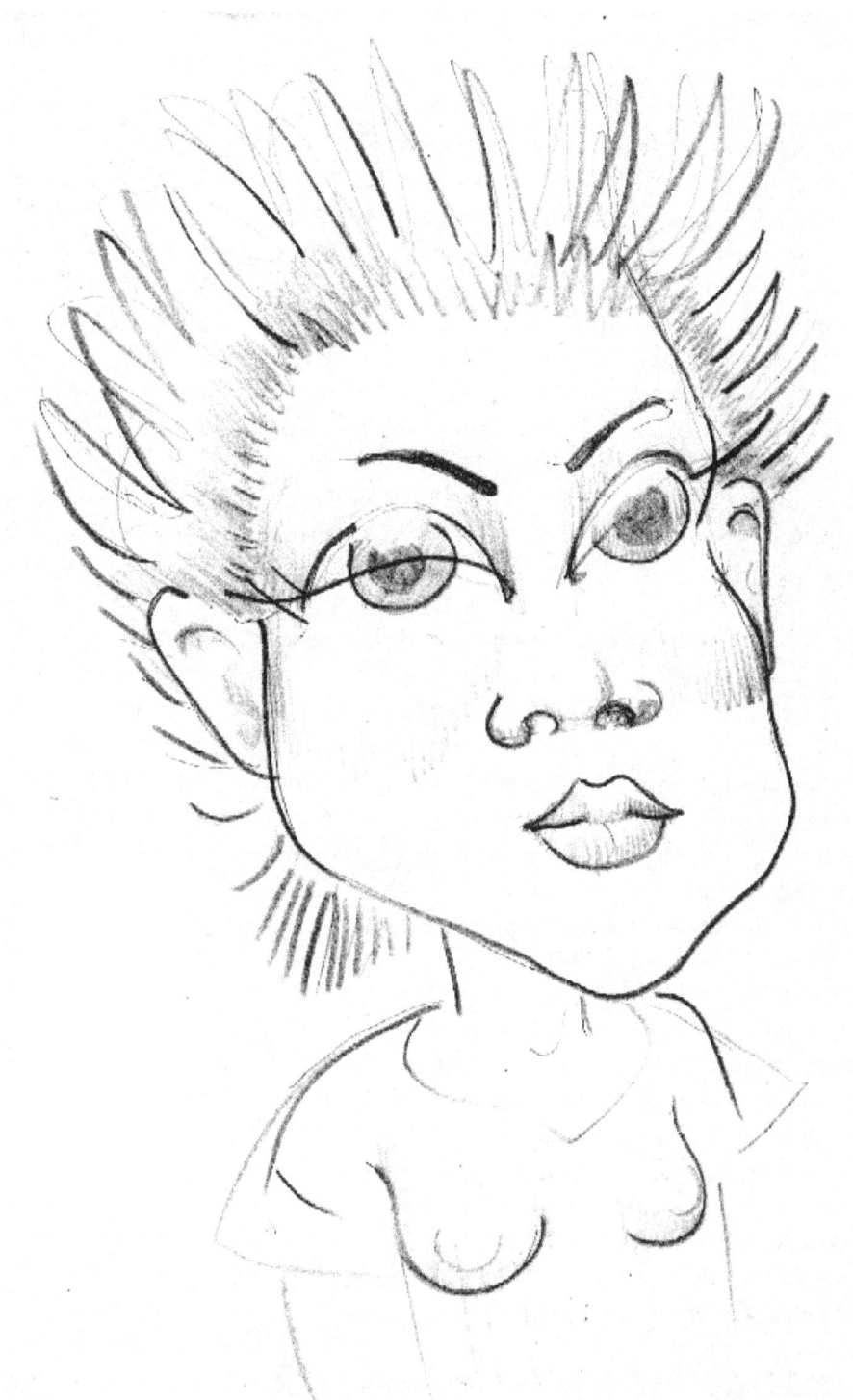

Calmer, not as frantic as Miss Bug-Eyes

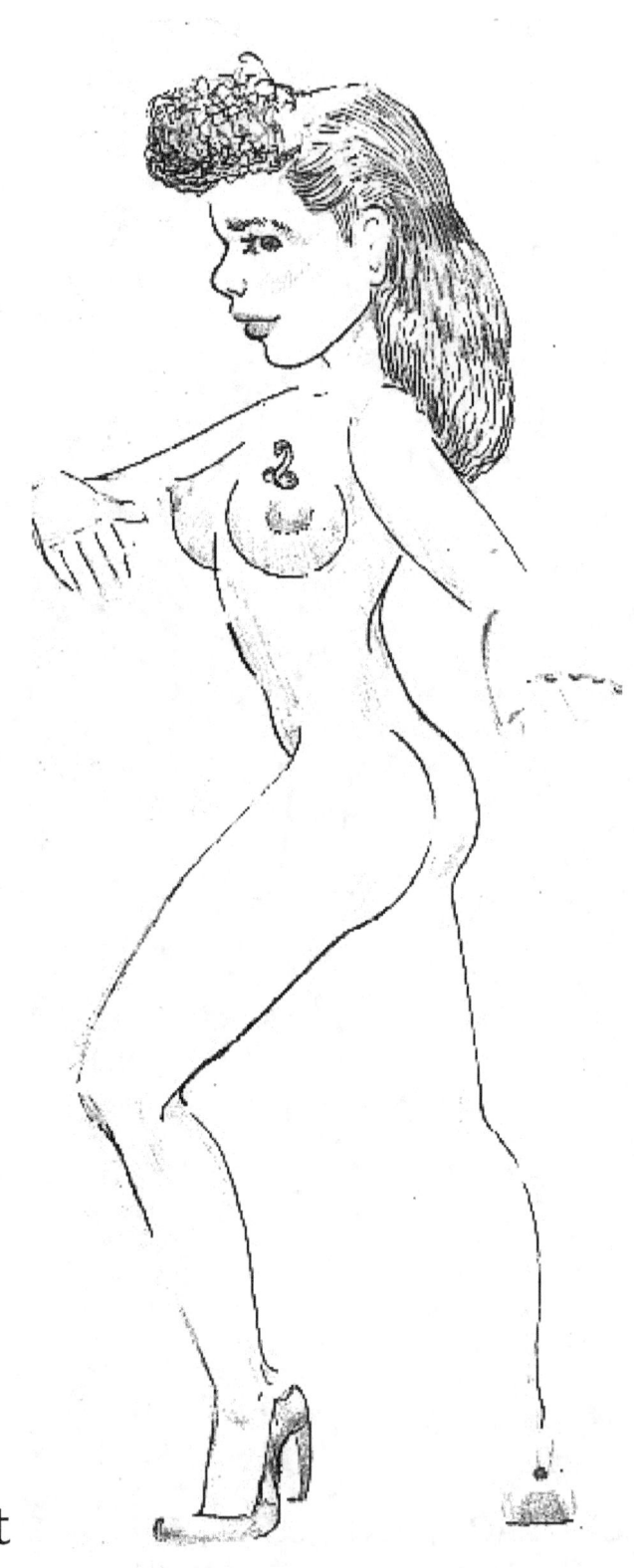

Yes, that was
a COBRA tattoo
over her heart...
Miss CobraHeart

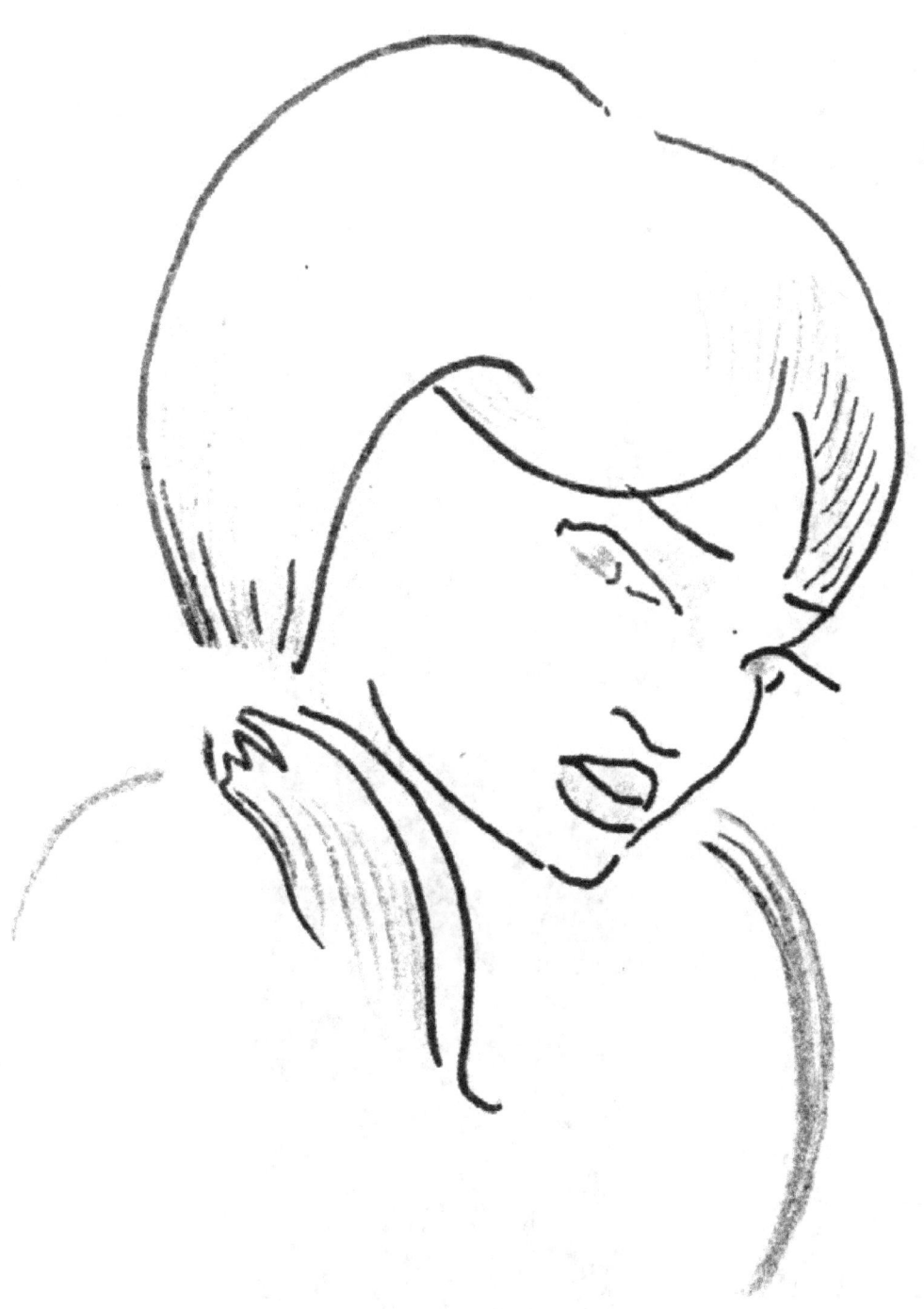

I suspect she was Vietnamese...

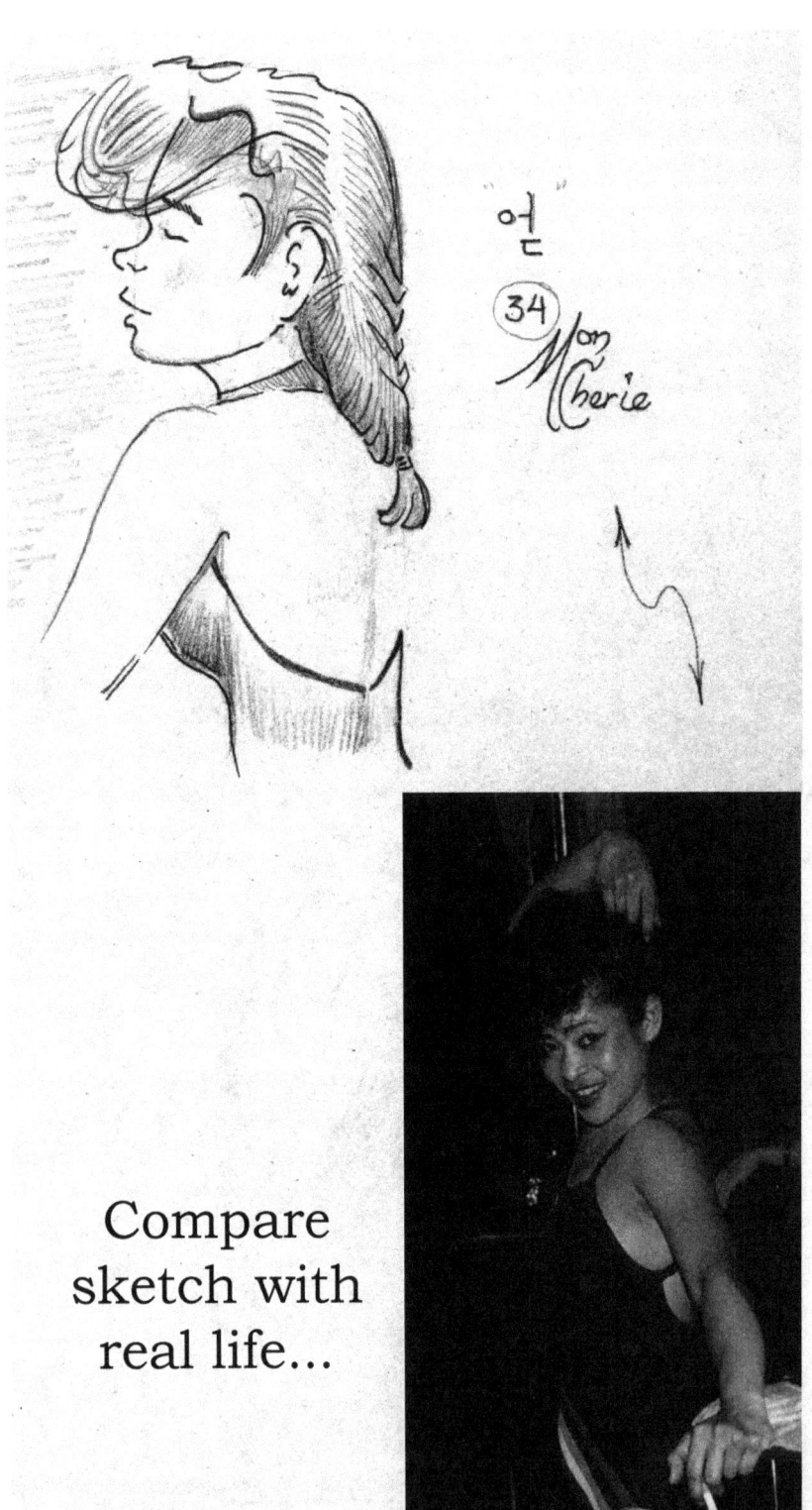

"얼"

(34) Mon Cherie

Compare
sketch with
real life...

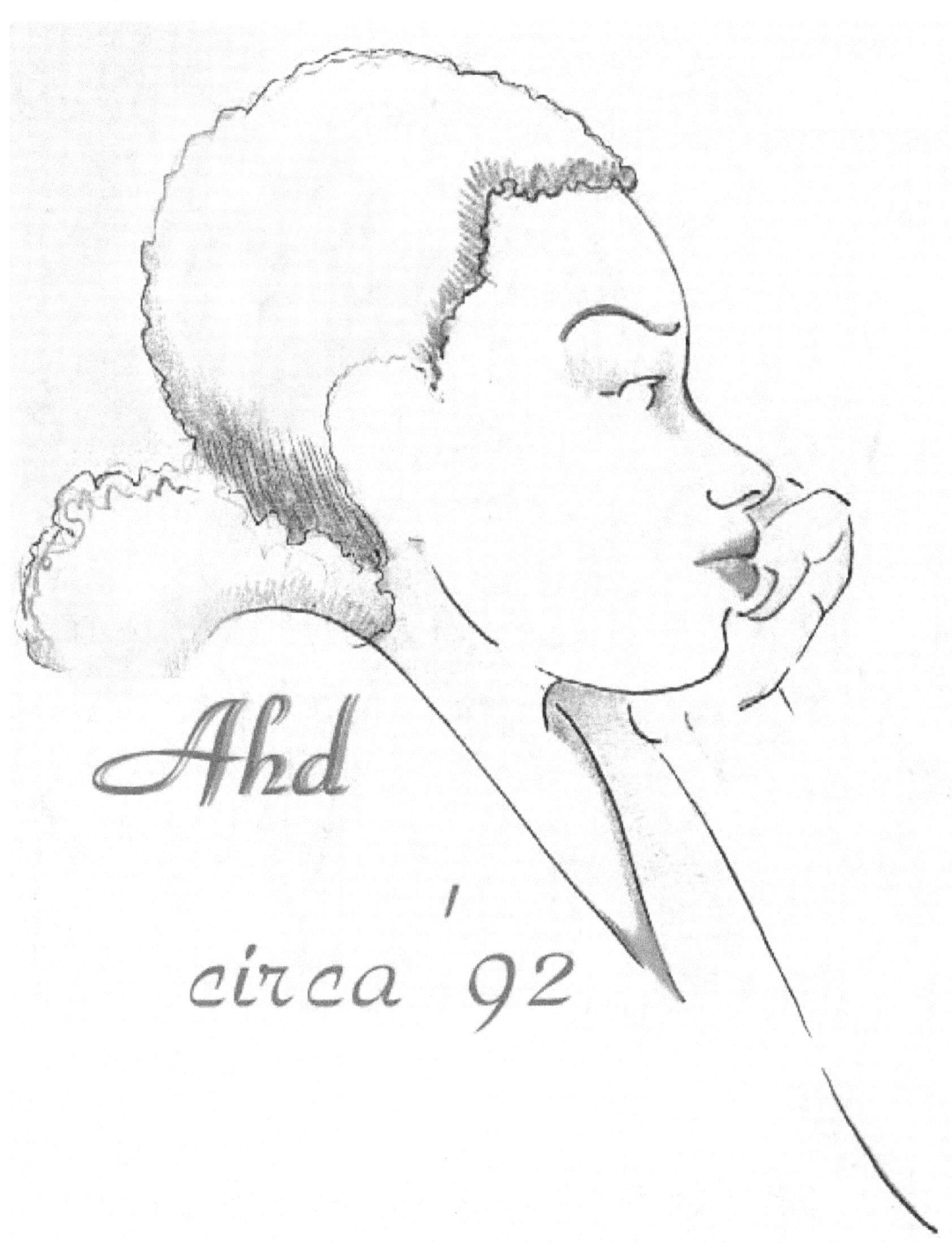

Ahd

circa '92

I loved the graceful black-Thai lines...

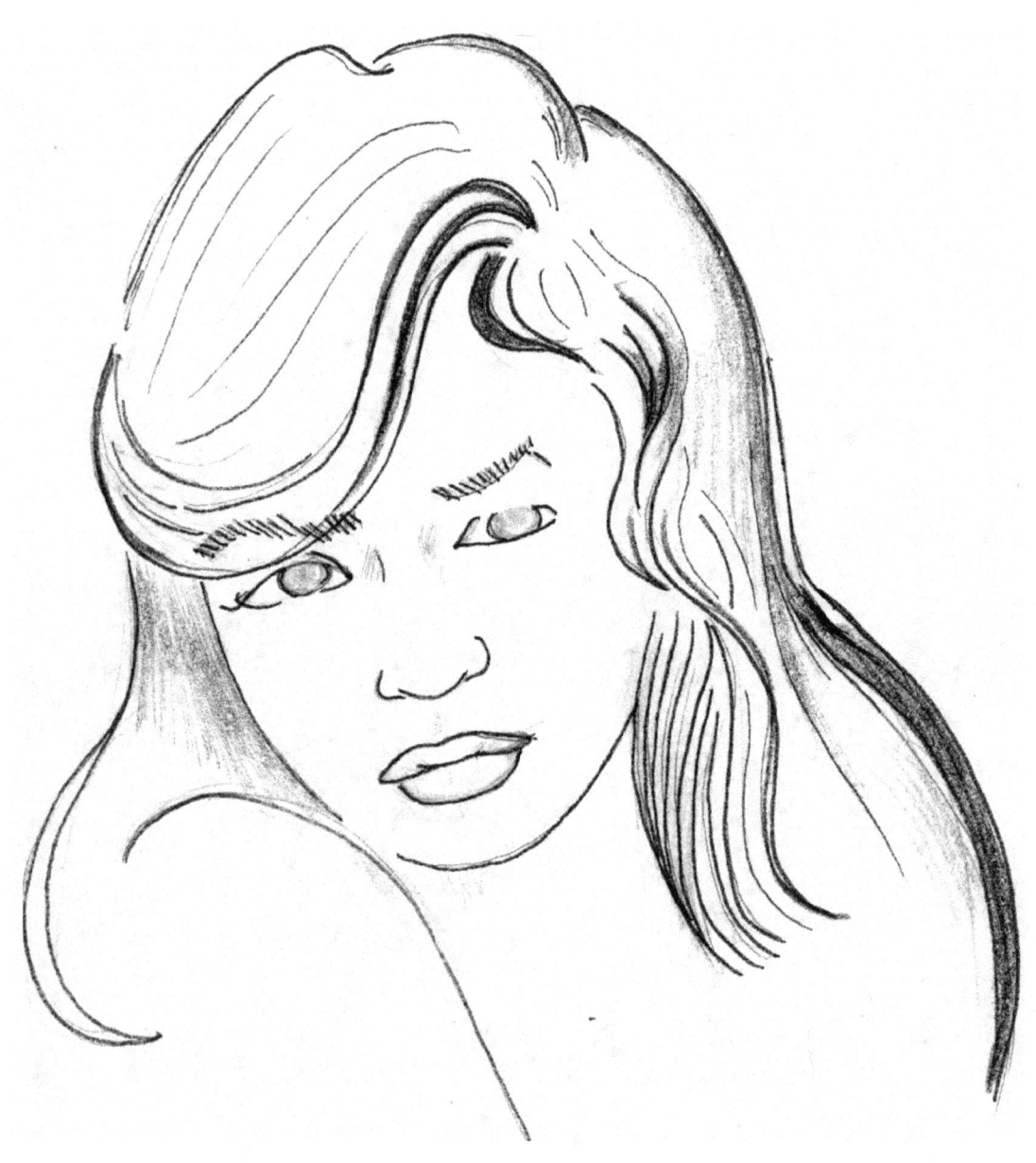

She danced at 'Crazy Cats' in
Soi Cowboy (Soi K'boi)

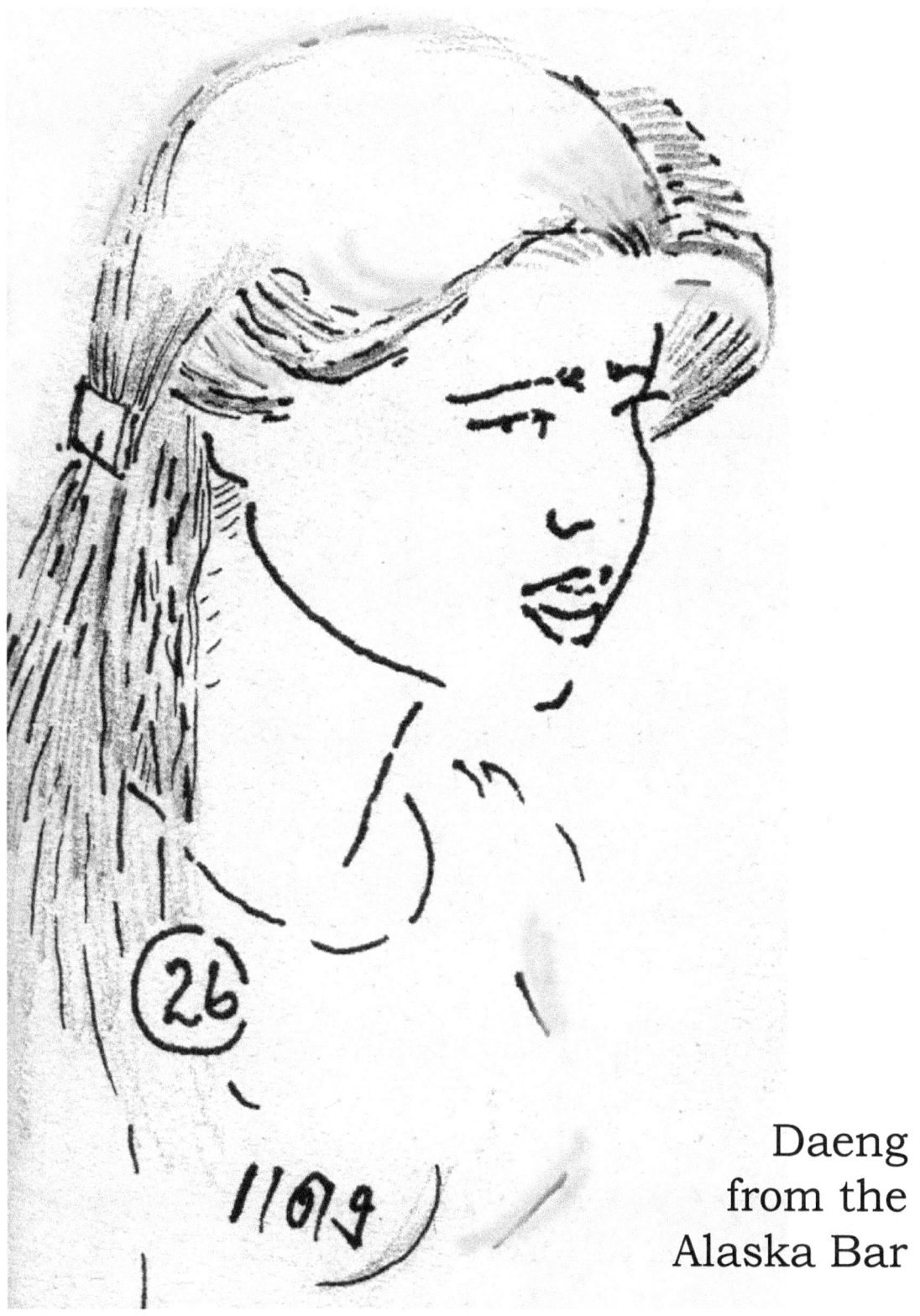

Daeng
from the
Alaska Bar

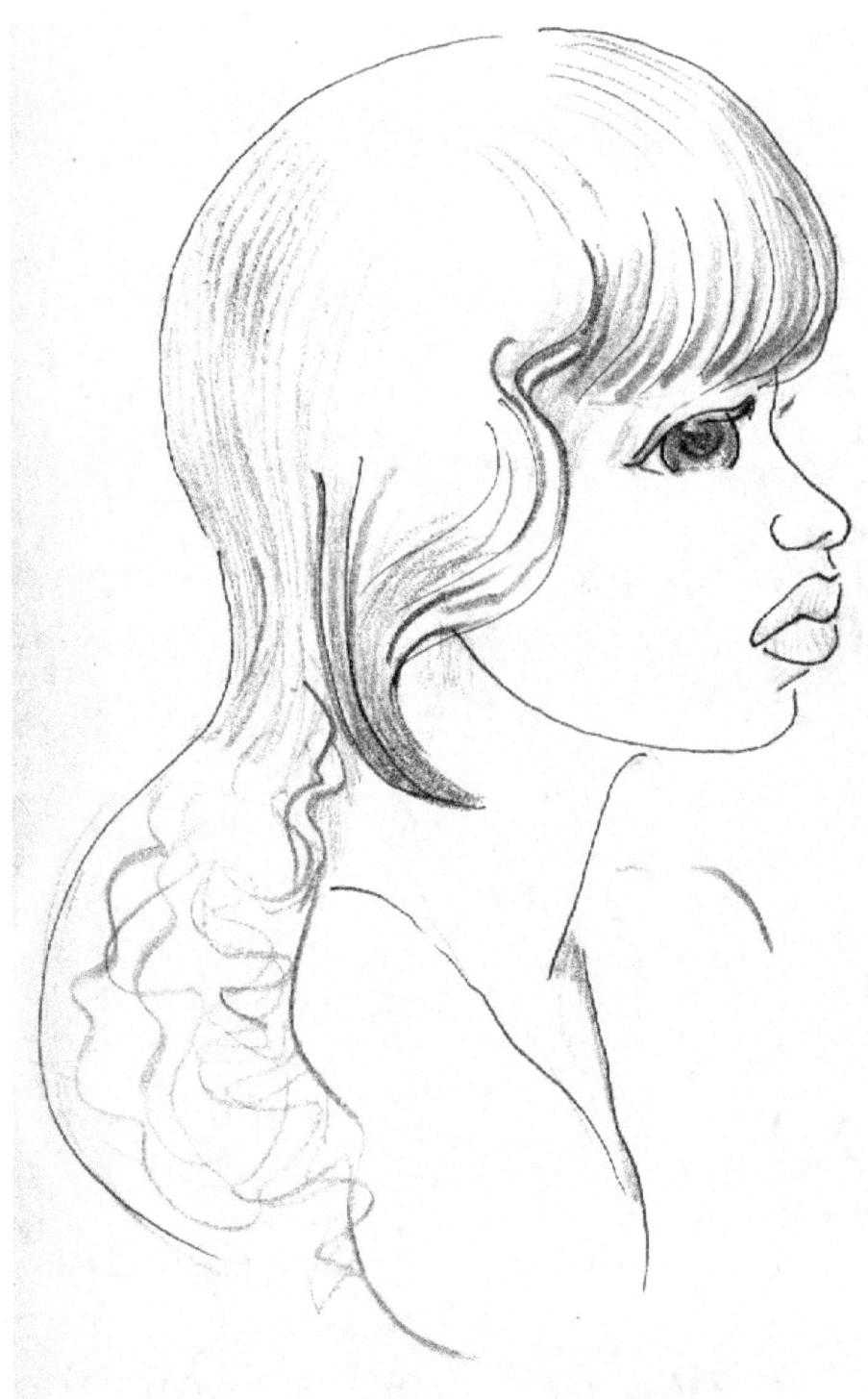

A different 'Daeng'...

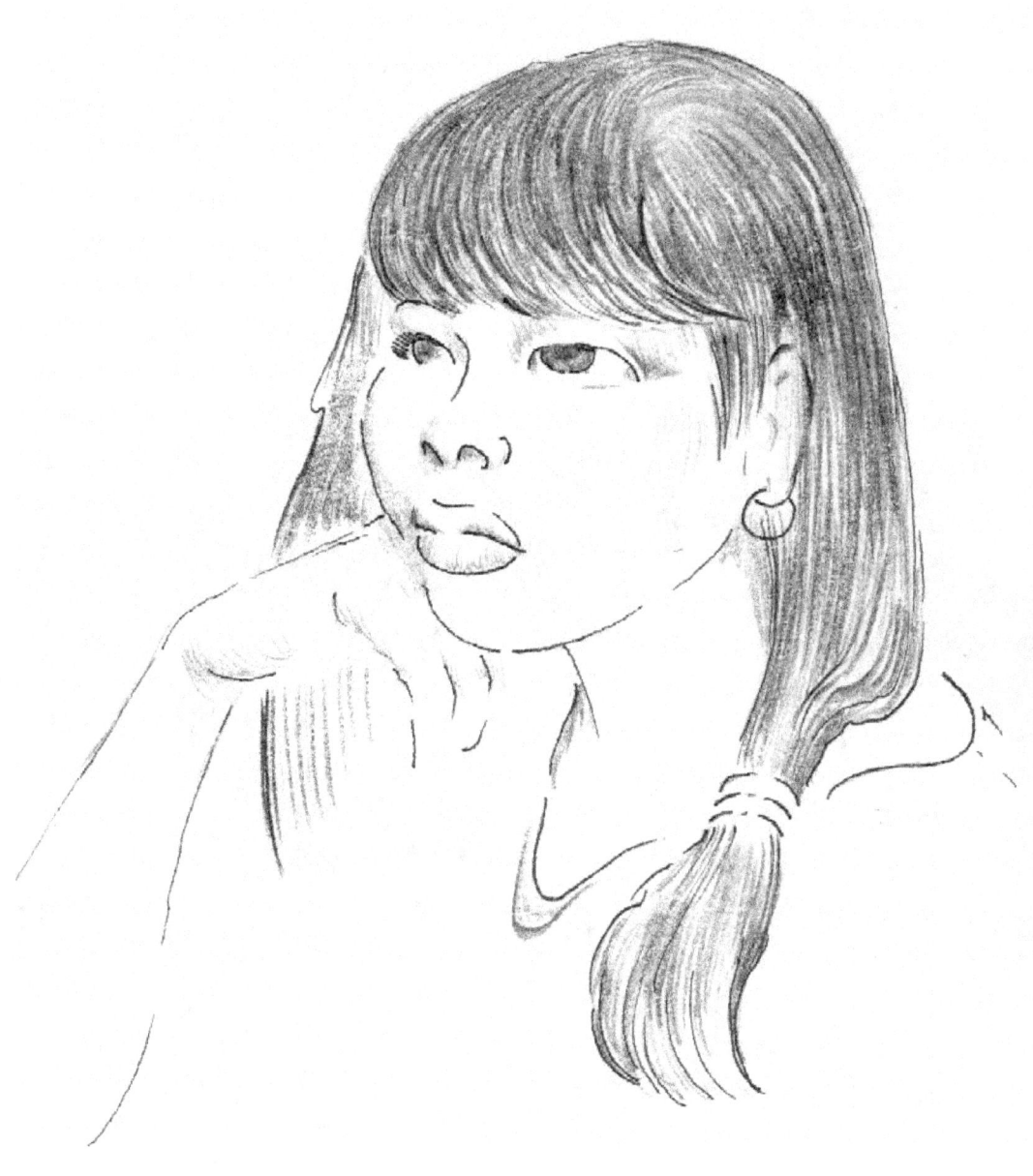

Miss Dahm, dancing in a Bangkok
establishment.

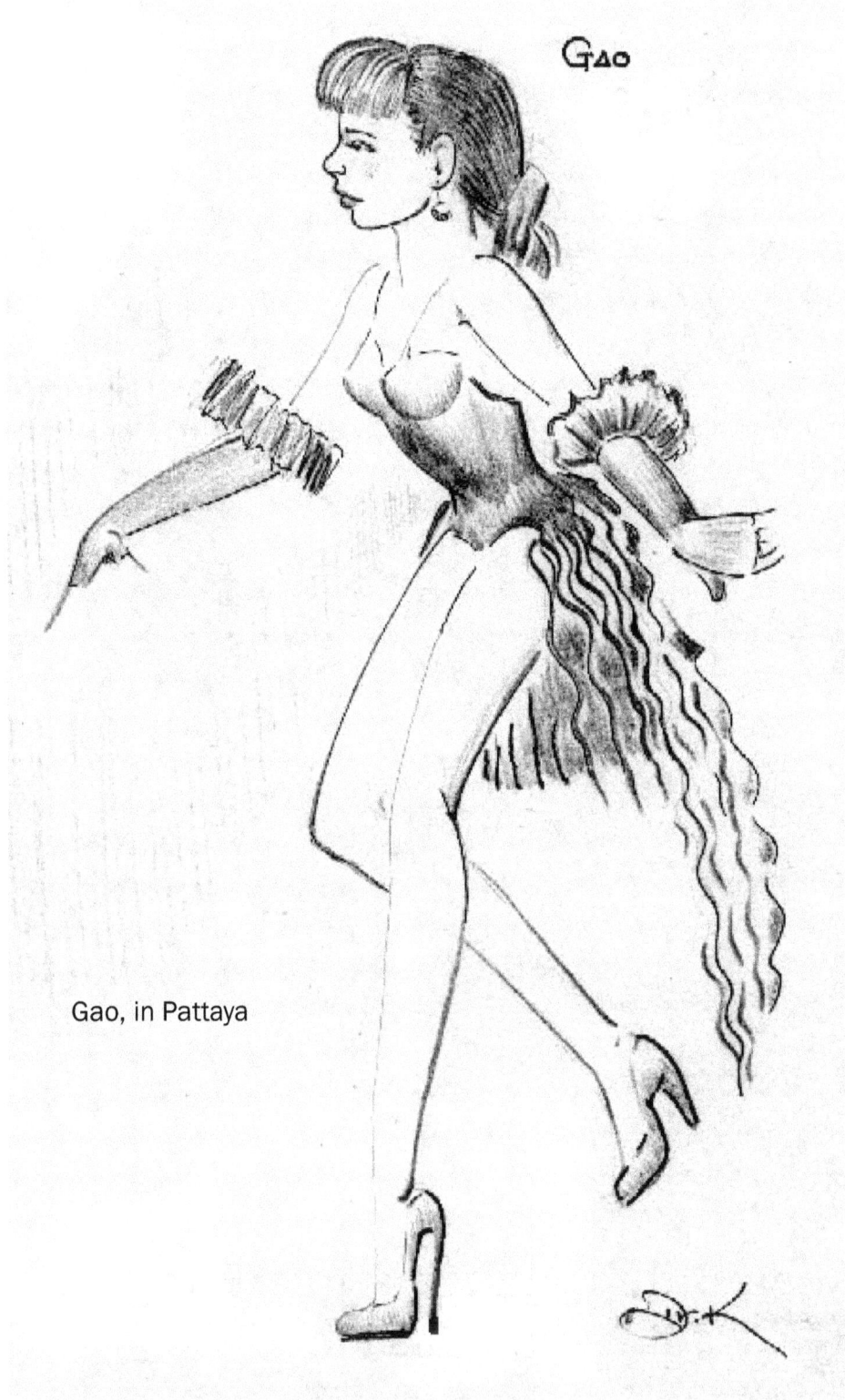

Gao, in Pattaya

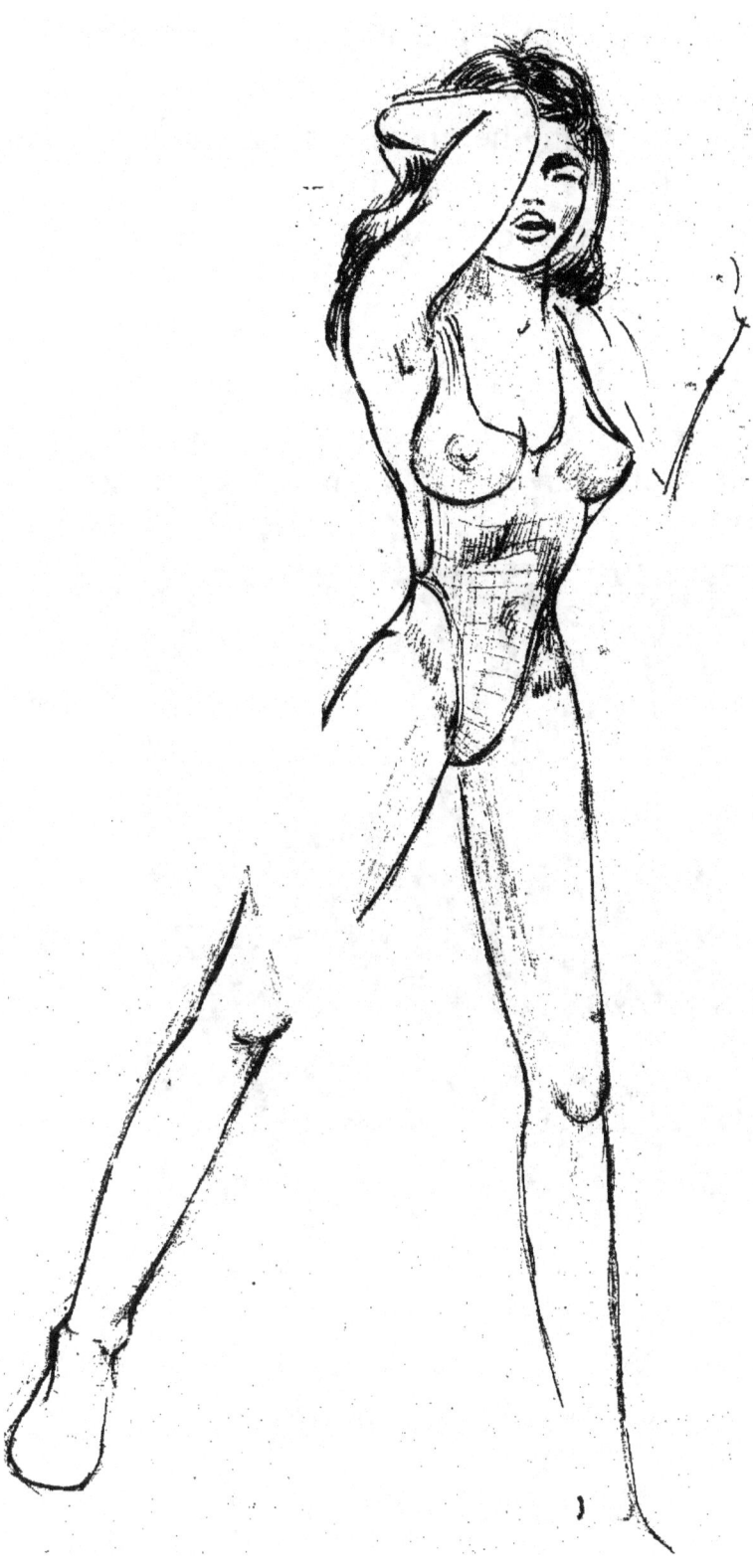

Miss Frog

Appendix: After Words

-Miss Apple, page one, was riding her motorcycle home from work at 0330 one morning, and drove at speed into the grill of an on-coming truck. Police asked me to identify the body so they could call the family.

-Baby GoGo may have been Pattaya's most lucrative bar, but if so, it was in part because the owner sold SHARES at $10,000 a share; to Euro and Aussie and American investors... hundreds of them, until somebody got wise...

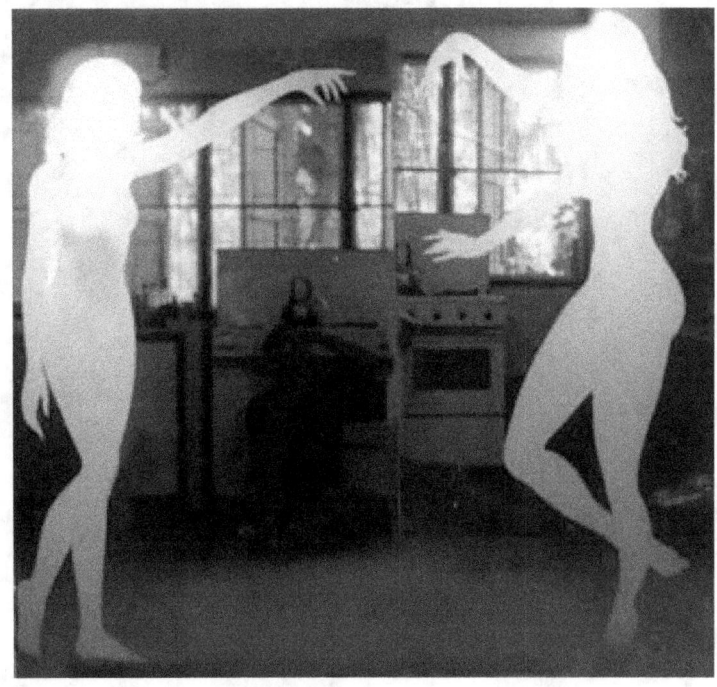

These are the mirrors I designed for Baby's interior.

+Answer to a Frequently Asked Question: No, I did NOT 'sample the delights' of the ladies drawn and sketched here..

+Yes, some are *caricatures* and some are sketch-portraits.

People Dreams #2: *The Dancers*

An Adult Coloring Book

Not rated XXX or XX or X or even PG (Parental Guidance)... this is *almost* family suitable, but since it does show professional dancers in various lovely stages of undress, it is probably NSFW.

So enjoy the subtle and overt pleasures of the human female form, as you add color and details to these line-drawings, pen-and-inks, done on-location in Pattaya and Bangkok, Thailand, by artist Karridine.

These are some of the faces and forms who danced across the life-path of Karridine, and now grace the pages of this coloring book.

Oh, and ONE of these drawings is of a *man*... can you guess *which* drawing?

For further info on carved-glass custom designs, or to order your lover's portrait in glass or mirror, contact
Karridine (at) **Gmail.com**

For a chance to help make the indie film 'Cleanup Crew', go to
http://bit.ly/1HCuLk9